MILNER CRAFT SERIES

Beautiful Boxes

TO CREATE, COVER AND DECORATE

JUDY NEWMAN

SALLY MILNER PUBLISHING

Dedication

Dedicated to the memory of Alice

First published in 1990 by
Sally Milner Publishing Pty Ltd
558 Darling Street
Rozelle NSW 2039 Australia

Reprinted 1990, 1991, 1992, 1993, 1994

© Judy Newman 1990

Production by Sylvana Scannapiego,
Island Graphics
Cover design by David Constable
Photography by Rodney Weidland
Illustrations by Louise McGeachie and John Karapatsas
Typeset in Goudy Old Style
by Asset Typesetting Pty Ltd
Printed in Singapore

National Library of Australia
Cataloguing-in-Publication data:

Newman, Judy.
  Beautiful boxes to create, cover and decorate.

  ISBN 1 86351 008 7.

  1.Box making. 2. Handicraft. 3. Boxes, Ornamental.
  I. Title. (Series: Milner Craft series).

745.593

CONTENTS

PAPER-DECORATED BOXES

There's nothing like a beautiful box to give a special quality to a gift! In this section the boxes are made from cardboard and tape, then covered in paper – they're easy and inexpensive. (See instructions starting on page 5.)

LARGE SQUARE BOX, ROUND BOX AND HEART BOX

OVAL BOX, HEXAGONAL BOX AND SMALL SQUARE BOX

RECTANGULAR BOX, BOOK BOX AND HEXAGONAL BOX WITH HINGED LID

BOX WITH DIVIDED LID

SET OF THREE BOXES WITH DROP-IN LIDS

BOX WITH ROLLED PAPER KNOB

COLLAGE BOX

BOX WITH CUT-OUT BOWS AND BOX WITH CUT-OUT DAISIES

TORN TISSUE-PAPER BOX

STATIONERY SET

DESK SET

INTRODUCTION

There's something about boxes – you just can't help wondering what's inside. But more than that, they're pretty, practical and provide stylish storage; they stack up, they make presents look so appealing, they decorate, hold jewellery and keep treasured mementos and love letters. And, you can work with many different crafts to decorate them.

From a few sheets of cardboard you can create truly beautiful boxes or box sets, in a wide variety of shapes and sizes. Or you can recycle an ordinary box into something quite exotic. The coverings can be embroidered, pleated, beaded, decoupaged, painted, collaged, patterned with cut-outs, patchworked or quilted.

I'm pleased to be able to share some of my ideas with you. Most of the boxes won't take more than a few hours to complete and I'm sure you'll love the results as much as I do. Above all, have fun with the projects in this book, then experiment with new ideas of your own.

TERMS USED IN THIS BOOK

Cut
Always use a sharp craft knife or scalpel to cut cardboard pieces. Make several cuts along the line, applying light pressure only; much easier than trying to force the knife through a sheet of cardboard.

Score
A light cut into the cardboard, but not through it! This keeps the sheet attached but allows it to be bent along the scored line. Always bend cardboard with the scored side out.

Glue
The choice is yours, unless a particular glue is indicated in the box instructions. Glue stick and spray adhesive are convenient and effective in most cases, but craft glue is sometimes called for. See notes in 'Materials and Equipment Needed'.

Grain
When making boxes with curved sides (round, oval or heart-shaped) work with the grain of the cardboard. Cardboard will bend more easily in one direction, due to the grain.

Ascertain which way the grain runs by flexing the sheet between your hands. Cut box pieces across the grain so they bend more easily.

MATERIALS AND EQUIPMENT NEEDED

Self-healing cutting mat
Protects table-top and provides a stable surface to cut paper and cardboard.

Craft knife or scalpel
For cutting paper and cardboard; change blades often. When cutting heavy cardboard it is easier to make several cuts along the line to be cut, rather than applying heavier pressure. Several light cuts will give a straighter line and make easier work.

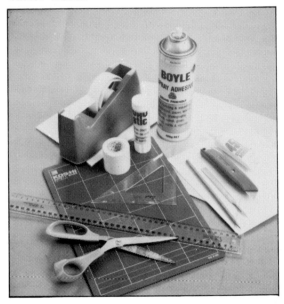

Materials and equipment

Ruler
For straight edges and accurate measurements. Clear plastic is easiest to work with although an 'M' shaped metal safety ruler will protect fingers.

Set square
Use the set square to check right angles – you'll make a neater, sturdier box with a well fitting lid if angles are true.

Scissors
For cutting fabric and clipping paper.

Pencils
To draw the box dimensions.

Tape
Use tape to hold the box components together. Where extra strength is needed, use a masking tape or packaging tape. Bookbinding tape is excellent where a 'hinge' is required between a box and lid. Otherwise wide adhesive tape is inexpensive and invisible under paper covers.

Glue stick
Excellent for adhering paper, fabric and cardboard, giving a strong bond without causing ripples. It is convenient, easy-to-use and non-messy. Glue stick does not adhere immediately, allowing the surfaces to be re-adjusted for a perfect join.

Spray adhesive
Gives a strong bond and dries quickly. Always use in a well ventilated area, preferably outdoors. For a permanent bond, coat both surfaces to be joined.

Craft glue
A clear-drying craft glue is useful for sticking braid onto fabric and box edges to box base where a strong bond is required.

Light cardboard
Use light, flexible cardboard for curved parts of a round box, such as the walls and lid rim. Also use light cardboard for box walls; it is easy to cut and inexpensive.

Heavy cardboard
Pasteboard, box board or screen board is available from art supply shops or stationers in various weights. Heavy cardboard is required for box bases and lids where the rigidity and sturdiness are needed.

Paper
Gift wrap, tissue paper, stationery paper and handmade Japanese papers were used in this book.

Gift wrap is available in a wonderful array of colours and patterns.

Tissue paper can be used in layers to build up deeper shades of colour, and crumpled to line gift boxes.

Where plain paper is needed, try brown wrapping paper or stationery sheets.

And for a really special cover, use handmade paper. Handmade Japanese paper is very strong and is available in textured patterns, variegated dyes and with fibres, threads and even plant material embedded in the sheet.

Fabric
Natural fibres are easiest to work with, especially cotton. Try cottage prints, patchwork calicos and lightweight furnishing fabrics; they have lovely patterns and colours.

Wadding
Thin polyester wadding can be used under fabric to pad and soften the box lines. Glue wadding to cardboard first, trim to the cardboard shape, then cover with fabric.

Twisted thread
To make a twisted thread cord, take a length of embroidery thread (Perle Cotton works well). Tape one end to a table or have someone hold it for you. Twist from the other end, then pick the thread up halfway along its length. The two halves will twist around each other, making a cord.

How to draw a square, circle or hexagon

Circle
Use a compass, or simply draw around a jar, saucer, dinner plate or frying pan – whichever is closer to the size you want!

Square
Draw a line to the length you require the sides of the square to be. Use a set square to draw a line at a perfect 90 degree angle at each end of the first line, and extend these lines to the measurement of the first line. Check the angles and draw in the final side.

Hexagon
Actual size diagrams are provided for all hexagonal boxes in this book except for the Easy Hat Box. For this box, or to vary the size of other hexagonal boxes, trace the hexagon pattern from the hexagon box diagram on page 11 onto paper. Cut out the hexagon and glue it to the centre of the cardboard sheet you will be using to make the box.

Draw diagonal lines through opposite points of the hexagon, extending them out from the original hexagon. Measure the distance between these lines to find the desired wall distance and draw in the new actual-size hexagon.

See Heart Box and Oval Box instructions for how to draw a heart or an oval.

Tips

Check the lids fit and sides are same height before covering with fabric or paper. At this stage they can easily be trimmed to fit precisely.

When recycling boxes, first cover them with plain white paper to hide any bright colours or writing.

Beautiful covering need not be expensive gift wrap. Try covering boxes in newspaper, plain brown paper, foil or pre-used tissue paper. Decorate plain papers with paint or crayon.

And trims can be string, braid or wool – experiment!

Or use corrugated cardboard to make your box and then spray paint it.

Use the instructions and diagrams provided to learn the basic principles, then design your own box. Try making a huge storage box by varying the dimensions of one of the projects in this book. Or draw an unusual shape, say a five-sided figure and follow the principles learned to make it into a box complete with lid.

The detailed step-by-step pictures which are included with the instructions for the padded hat box will be useful as a guide to constructing other boxes too.

Note

Diagrams are mostly not actual size, but give the measurements for each shape to be cut. Conversions from metric to inches are not always exact, but are approximations that give the correct proportions.

PAPER-DECORATED BOXES

LARGE SQUARE BOX

YOU WILL NEED:
heavy cardboard
light cardboard
paper
spray adhesive or glue stick
ribbon
tape

250/10″

A

250/10″

250/10″

248/9¾″

B

248/9¾″

248/9¾″

250/10″   250/10″   250/10″   250/10″

32/1¼″   C

248/9¾″   248/9¾″   248/9¾″   248/9¾″

D

185/7¼″

All measurements in millimetres/inches

1. Cut A, B, C and D to measurements shown on diagrams. Cut A and B from heavy cardboard and C and D from light cardboard. Score C and D along broken lines. (If piece of cardboard you are using to cut C and D is not long enough, join two pieces with tape at one of the scored lines.)

2. Fold C (lid rim) around A (lid top) and tape the edges of C and A together tightly at right angles to each other, continuing until the rim ends meet. Tape the rim ends together to form a corner.

3. Attach D (box wall) to B (box base) using the same method as above.

4. To cover lid, cut paper strip 20 mm/1″ wider than the rim. Glue to rim so that 10 mm/½″ of paper hangs free at top and bottom edge of rim. At each corner of top paper allowance, use scissors to clip paper up to the edge of cardboard. Fold and glue paper allowances onto the lid and inside the rim. Use the same method to cover the box walls.

5. Cut a same-size paper square for lid top. Glue in position.

6. To add the finishing touch, tie the box with wide satin ribbon and top with a bow.

Note: If you wish to line the box, cover the inside (unscored side) of each piece before assembling the box.

ROUND BOX

625/24¼"

35/1½" C

190/7½"
A

YOU WILL NEED:
heavy cardboard
light cardboard
paper spray adhesive or glue stick

610/24"

D

135/5½"

B
188/7¼"

All measurements in millimetres/inches

1. Cut A, B, C and D to measurements shown on diagrams. Cut A (lid top) and B (box base) from heavy cardboard. Cut C (lid rim) and D (box walls) from light cardboard, cutting the length of these strips across the grain of the cardboard (see note page 1) so they bend easily into a cylinder.
Note: To vary size of the box trace around a dinner plate or any round object to make piece A; make B 2 mm/¼" smaller in diameter than A and cut C and D the width you desire and 20 mm/1" longer than the circumferences of A and B.

Steps 2 to 4 are illustrated in the Padded Hat Box instructions, see page 37.

2. Attach a strip of tape along one long edge as C, allowing half the width of the tape to hang free from the edge.

3. Use scissors to clip V-shapes out of the tape every 15 mm/½".

4. Hold A next to the edge of C that has tape attached so that adhesive side of tape faces in towards circle. Keeping the edges of each piece tightly together at right angles, press the first piece of tape onto the circle. Roll the card strip around the circle, pressing each piece of tape across onto the circle so the strip sits flush with the circle edge. When ends of the strip meet, overlap ends and tape together firmly.

5. Use the same method as above to attach D (box wall) to B (box base).

6. Cut a strip of paper the same length as C but 20 mm/1" wider. Glue it around lid rim so that 10 mm/½" of paper hangs free at top and bottom edge. Glue bottom allowance of paper to the inside of lid rim. Use scissors to clip V-shapes from the top allowance of paper every 15 mm/½". Glue the clipped edge onto lid top.

7. Cut a circle of paper the same size as A and glue onto the lid top.

8. Cover the bottom of box using the same method as for the lid.

Note: If you wish to line the box, this can be done by covering the inside of each piece before assembling the box.

Ribbons can be glued around the edge of the lid for decoration or add a ribbon bow to the top of the box.

HEART BOX

YOU WILL NEED:
heavy cardboard
light cardboard
paper
spray adhesive or glue stick

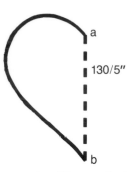

a

130/5″

b

All measurements in millimetres/inches

1. To make a heart pattern, fold a piece of paper in half and draw a half heart shape, using the diagram as a guide and drawing to the measurements indicated (you can vary these measurements for a larger or smaller heart). Cut out, leaving folded edge uncut, then open up and use as pattern.

2. Use this pattern to cut two heart shapes from heavy cardboard, one for the lid top and one for the base. Trim 2 mm/¼″ off the base, all around.

3. From light cardboard, cut two 35 mm/1½″ wide strips for lid rim; make each strip about 20 mm/1″ longer than the measurement around half the lid, i.e. around the curved edge of the lid top from point 'a' to point 'b'.

4. Also cut from light cardboard two 90 mm/3½″ wide strips for the box wall; make each strip about 20 mm/1″ longer than the measurement around half the base heart.

5. Place a piece of tape along one long edge of one lid rim piece, allowing half the tape to hang free from the edge. Use scissors to clip small V-shapes from the tape. Position the edge of the lid rim that has tape attached so that the end of the rim is at the top point of the heart. The adhesive part of the tape should face inwards. Hold lid heart and rim together tightly at right angles to each other and pull the free edge of the tape across the lid heart and press it in place. Continue until the bottom point of the heart is reached. Trim the lid rim in line with the bottom point of the heart, making sure you cut at right angles.

6. Use the same method to attach the other half of the lid rim. Trim the rim ends (remember to make sure rim ends are cut at right angles, otherwise the lid won't fit the box). Tape the ends together securely.

7. Repeat steps 5 and 6 to attach the walls to the base.

8. Cover with paper using the same method as that described in steps 6 to 8 for the Round Box, but using separate strips of paper to cover each side of the lid and box wall.

OVAL BOX

YOU WILL NEED:
heavy cardboard
light cardboard
paper
cord or twisted thread
spray adhesive or glue stick

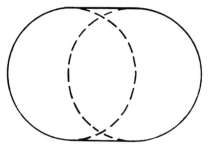

How to draw an oval

1. Use the diagram included as a guide to drawing an oval. Position two small plates on a piece of paper as shown in the diagram. Trace around each one and then draw a line across the top and bottom to form an oval. Use this pattern to cut two ovals from heavy cardboard, one for the lid and one for the base.

2. Trim 2 mm/¼″ off the base, all around. Cut a strip from light cardboard for the box wall; the width of the strip will determine the height of the box (ours is 100 mm/4″); make the length of the strip 20 mm/1″ longer than the circumference of the box base (the smaller oval). For the lid rim cut a strip to the width desired (ours is 25 mm/1″) and 20 mm/1″ longer than the circumference of the lid (the larger oval).

3. Attach a strip of tape along one long edge of the lid rim, allowing half the tape to hang free from the edge. Use scissors to clip V-shapes out of the tape every 15 mm/½″. Using the edge of the rim that has tape attached, bend the rim around the large oval so that the adhesive side of tape faces inwards. Keep the edges together and at right angles to each other. Pull the free edge of the tape across and press it onto the oval piece, keeping both pieces tightly together, and continuing until rim ends meet. Trim the narrow ends of the lid rim so they overlap 10 mm/½″, then tape securely.

4. Use the same procedure as above to attach the box base and the box wall.

5. Cover the box following steps 6 to 8 of the Round Box on page 7.

6. Using a skewer or large needle, pierce a hole at each end of the box wall, about 25 mm/1″ from the top edge. Insert one end of a length of cord through each hole from the outside of the box and tape it to the inside.

Note: If you wish to line the box, cover each cardboard piece with paper before assembling the box.

SMALL SQUARE BOX

Following the diagram for the Large Square Box on page 6, make piece A (lid) 55 mm/2¼″ square; B (base) 53 mm/2″ square; C (lid rim) 15 mm/¾″ wide and each length 55 mm/2¼″; D (box walls) 55 mm/2¼″ wide and each length 53 mm/2″.

Make and cover the box following the same procedure as for Large Square Box.

HEXAGONAL BOX

60/2⅜″ 60/2⅜″ 60/2⅜″ 60/2⅜″ 60/2⅜″ 60/2⅜″

30/1¼″ C

YOU WILL NEED:
heavy cardboard
paper
spray adhesive or glue stick

55/2⅛″ 55/2⅛″ 55/2⅛″ 55/2⅛″ 55/2⅛″ 55/2⅛″

72/3″ D

All measurements in millimetres/inches

1. Cut A and B using tracings of actual-size hexagonal shapes provided, and C and D to measurements shown on diagrams. Cut all from heavy cardboard. Score along broken lines.

2. Fold C (rim) around A (lid) and tape pieces together tightly at right angles to each other (it is easiest to do this by holding edges of C tightly against A one by one and taping each edge in place). Tape ends of C together where they meet to form a corner.

3. Cut a strip of paper 20 mm/1″ wider than C and 10 mm/½″ longer than the circumference of C. Glue the paper around C so that 10 mm/½″ of paper hangs free at top and bottom edge of rim. At each corner, use scissors to clip paper up to edge of cardboard. Glue top allowance of paper onto the lid and bottom allowance inside the rim. Cut a hexagon slightly smaller than A and glue to the lid top.

4. Follow the same procedure as in steps 2 and 3 to make and cover the box, using pieces B (base) and D (walls).

Note: To line the box, cover the inside (unscored side) of each piece before assembling the box.

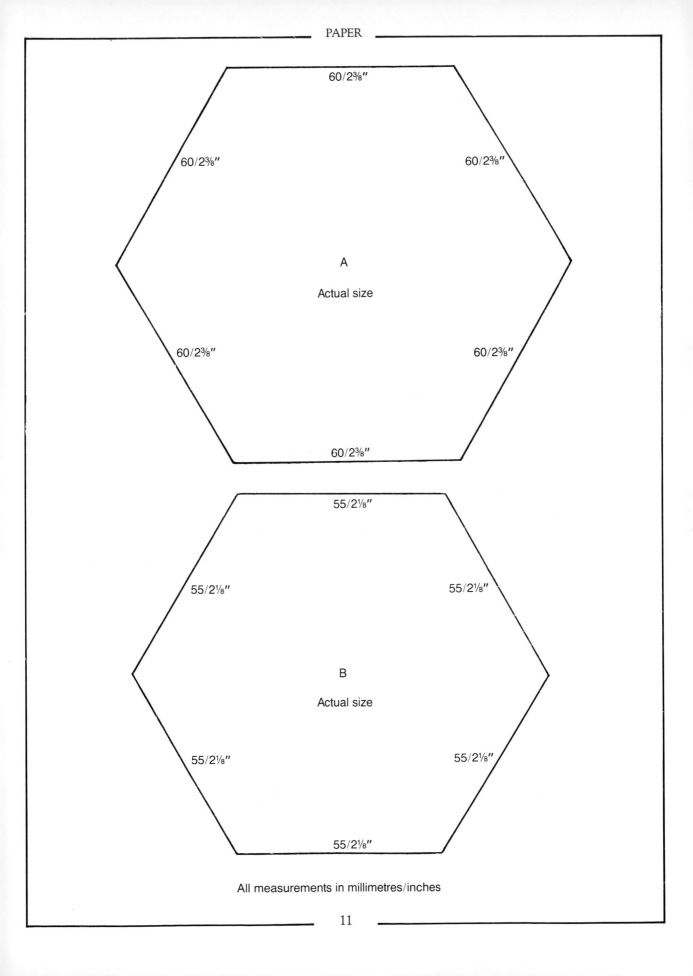

60/2⅜"

60/2⅜"

60/2⅜"

A

Actual size

60/2⅜"

60/2⅜"

60/2⅜"

55/2⅛"

55/2⅛"

55/2⅛"

B

Actual size

55/2⅛"

55/2⅛"

55/2⅛"

All measurements in millimetres/inches

RECTANGULAR BOX

YOU WILL NEED:
heavy cardboard
light cardboard
paper
four brass corners
spray adhesive or glue stick
cord (optional)

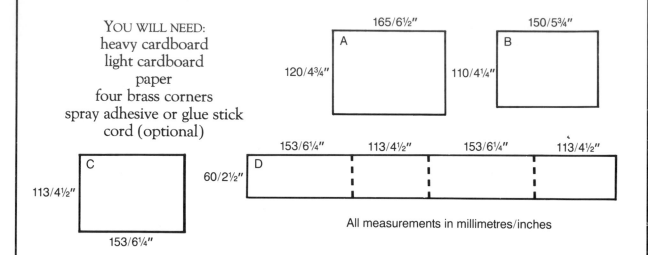

All measurements in millimetres/inches

1. Cut A, B, C and D to measurements shown on diagrams. Cut A, B and C from heavy cardboard and D from light cardboard. Score along broken lines.

2. Cut pieces of paper the same size as C and D and glue in place on one side of C and D (cover unscored side of D).

3. Fold D (walls) around C (base) so that covered side faces inwards. Tape the edges of D and C together tightly at right angles to each other (it is easiest to do this by holding edges of D tightly against C one by one and taping each edge in place). Tape ends of D together where they meet to form a corner.

4. Cut a strip of paper 20 mm/1″ wider and 20 mm/1″ longer than the circumference of D. Glue paper around D so that 10 mm/½″ of paper hangs free at top and bottom edge. At each corner of bottom paper allowance, use scissors to clip the paper up to the edge of cardboard. Fold and glue paper allowances onto the base and to inside of walls.

5. Cut a piece of paper 10 mm/½″ larger on all sides than A (lid). Glue onto A so that 10 mm/½″ of paper hangs free at each edge of A. Use scissors to clip out a small square of paper at each corner. Fold and glue the paper allowances to inside of A.

6. Use the same method as above to cover B (lid liner), then glue B onto the centre of A, uncovered sides together.

7. Press brass corners onto A and glue or squeeze them to hold in place.

8. Tie the box with cord.

BOOK BOX

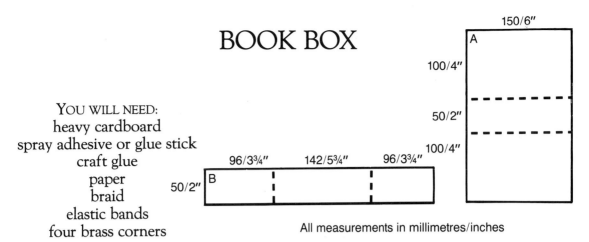

YOU WILL NEED:
heavy cardboard
spray adhesive or glue stick
craft glue
paper
braid
elastic bands
four brass corners

All measurements in millimetres/inches

1. Cut A and B from heavy cardboard to measurements shown on diagrams. Score along broken lines.

2. Cut a piece of paper the same size as B and glue in place on inside (unscored side) of B (box wall).

3. To cover outside of B, cut a piece of paper so that it is flush with B along one long edge and along both ends, but has an extra 10 mm/½″ along the remaining long edge (this will be the top edge). Glue paper on outside of B, folding and gluing 10 mm/½″ paper allowance to inside of B.

4. Glue braid over the paper edge on inside of wall from end to end.

5. Cut a piece of paper so that it is 15 mm/1″ larger on all sides than A. Glue onto outside (scored side) of A so that 15 mm/1″ of paper hangs free at each edge of A, leaving paper loose enough to allow A to fold up. Use scissors to clip out a small square of paper at each corner. Fold and glue the paper allowances to inside of A. (The three sections of A will form box base, back wall and lid.)

6. Cut inside paper cover about 10 mm/½″ smaller on all sides than A. Glue paper to the inside of A so that it is centred.

7. Apply craft glue to outer edges of both ends of B and to the outer bottom edge of B. Place wall carefully onto one end of A (this will be the base section), positioning it to sit 4 mm/⅛″ in from the edge all around.

8. Fold A over B and slip elastic bands around box to keep in position as it dries.

9. Leave to dry with a book on top as a weight, checking and adjusting wall position before glue sets.

10. Glue brass corners in place on A or squeeze gently with cloth-covered pliers to hold them in position.

Note: If your box lid won't sit flat, score the spine a little deeper.

HEXAGONAL BOX WITH HINGED LID

YOU WILL NEED:
heavy cardboard
light cardboard
paper
spray adhesive or glue stick
5 cm/2″ cord

55/2⅛″ 55/2⅛″ 55/2⅛″ 55/2⅛″ 55/2⅛″ 55/2⅛″

55/2⅛″ | C

All measurements in millimetres/inches

1. Cut A and B using tracings of actual-size hexagonal shapes provided on page 11, and C to measurements shown on diagram. Cut A and two B pieces from heavy cardboard and C from light cardboard. Score C along broken lines.

2. Cut one piece of paper so that it is 10 mm/½″ larger on all sides than A (lid) and one piece of paper so that it is 10 mm/½″ larger on all sides than one B piece (this will be lid liner). Glue paper on lid and liner so that 10 mm/½″ hangs free from edge on all sides. At each corner, use scissors to clip the paper up to the edge of cardboard. Fold and glue paper allowances to inside of lid and lid liner. Cover one side of the remaining B piece (base) with same-size piece of paper by gluing base to paper, then trimming paper flush with the edge. Cover the unscored side of C with same-size piece of paper.

3. Fold C (wall) around base B, covered side in, and tape the edges of C and B together tightly at right angles to each other (it is easiest to do this by holding edges of C tightly against B one by one and taping each edge in place). Tape ends of C together where they meet to form a corner.

4. Cut a strip of paper 20 mm/1″ wider and 20 mm/1″ longer than C. Glue it around the wall so that 10 mm/½″ of paper hangs free at the top and bottom edges and overlaps at the ends. Smooth out any wrinkles in the paper then fold and glue top paper allowance to inside of box. At each bottom corner, use scissors to clip paper up to edge of cardboard. Fold and glue paper allowance onto base.

5. Hold lid, covered side out, at right angles to box along one side and tape along this one side only, to form a hinge. Cut a piece of paper larger than the tape and glue it over the tape to conceal the hinge.

6. Tie a knot at one end of the cord. Tape the other end at front edge of lid.

7. Glue the remaining B piece (lid liner) onto the centre of A, uncovered sides together. Press A and B firmly together for a few seconds or hold with pegs until the glue dries.

SET OF THREE BOXES WITH DROP-IN LIDS

YOU WILL NEED:
heavy cardboard (see step 1)
paper
cord or twisted thread
spray adhesive or glue stick

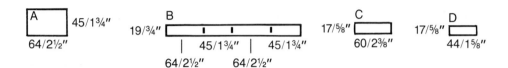

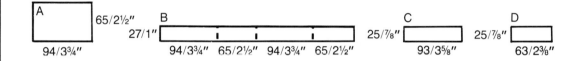

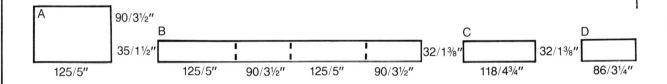

All measurements in millimetres/inches

1. Cut all pieces from cardboard to measurements shown on diagrams (for the larger box cardboard up to 2 mm/⅛″ thick will work well; for the smaller boxes 1 mm/¹⁄₁₆″ thick cardboard is best). Cut two A pieces for each box (lid and base). Cut two C and D pieces for each box. Score the B pieces along broken lines.

2. Cover one side of base A with same-size piece of paper (glue A to the wrong side of paper, then trim paper flush with A edges). The covered side will be the inside of box base.

3. Fold B (walls) around base A, covered side in, and tape edges tightly together at right angles to each other (it is easiest to do this by holding edges of B tightly against A one by one and taping each edge in place). Tape ends of B together where they meet to form a corner.

4. Cut a strip of paper 20 mm/1″ wider and 20 mm/1″ longer than B. Glue it around B so that 10 mm/½″ of paper hangs free at top and bottom edges and ends overlap. At each corner of bottom paper allowance, use scissors to clip the paper up to the edge of cardboard. Fold and glue the paper allowances onto the base and to inside of walls.

5. Cut a piece of paper 10 mm/½″ larger on all sides than the remaining A piece (lid). Glue onto A so that 10 mm/½″ of paper hangs free at each edge of A. Use scissors to clip out a small square of paper at each corner. Fold and glue the 10 mm/½″ paper allowance to the other side of lid (inside).

6. Pierce a hole through the centre of the lid. Cut a 8 cm/3″ length of cord and insert both ends through the hole from the covered side. Cover the ends with tape to insert them easily. Adjust the height of the cord loop and trim, then tape the ends onto the inside of the lid, as flat as possible. Cut a piece of paper slightly smaller than the lid and glue it to cover inside of lid.

7. Check that liner pieces (C and D) for each box fit neatly. If too large, trim to fit, then cut pieces of paper slightly larger than each C and D piece. Glue paper to each C and D piece so that equal amount of paper allowance remains on each side. Use scissors to clip out a small square of paper at each corner. Fold and glue the paper allowances to the inside of each liner piece, then glue each piece into the boxes, making sure you match the liners to the boxes to which they belong.

BOX WITH DIVIDED LID

YOU WILL NEED:
heavy cardboard
patterned and plain paper
narrow ribbon
spray adhesive or glue stick

This box is similar to the largest of the boxes in Set of Three Boxes with Drop-In Lids. Follow steps 1 to 4 of those instructions, using patterned paper for the outside coverings and plain for the linings.

5. Cut the remaining A piece (lid) in half across the width. Cut patterned pieces of paper 10 mm/½″ larger on all sides than the lid pieces. Glue onto each lid piece so that 10 mm/½″ of paper hangs free at each edge. Use scissors to clip out a small square of paper at each corner. Fold and glue the paper allowances to inside of lid pieces.

6. Tape the ends of a ribbon loop on the centre edge of each lid piece as pictured. Tape two lengths of ribbon on each outside edge of the lid pieces for hinges. Tape the other end of the ribbon hinges to the inside of the box. Cut plain pieces of paper slightly smaller than each lid piece and glue to cover inside lid.

7. Use the same method described in step 7 of Set of Three Boxes with Drop-In Lids to cover each of the lining pieces with plain paper and glue in place inside box.

BOX WITH PAPER KNOB

YOU WILL NEED:
heavy cardboard
paper (two colours)
spray adhesive or glue stick

1. Cut A, B and C to measurements shown on diagrams. Cut A and B from heavy cardboard and four C pieces from light cardboard. Score A along broken lines.

2. Cut a piece of paper the same size as the centre square of A (box base and walls) and glue in place on the centre square of A (unscored side). Fold up box sides and check each side is the same height; if not, trim the top edge to fit. Tape sides together at corners, making sure cardboard edges sit tightly together at right angles.

3. Cut a strip of paper 25 mm/1″ wider and 10 mm/½″ longer than the box wall circumference. Glue the paper around the box wall so that equal amounts of paper hang free at both top and bottom edge and ends overlap. Fold and glue top paper allowance to inside of box. At each corner of bottom allowance, use scissors to clip the paper up to the edge of cardboard. Fold and glue the bottom paper allowance onto base.

4. Glue a square of paper (cut slightly smaller than base) onto the base of box.

5. To cover lid (B), cut a square of paper 10 mm/½″ larger on all sides than lid. Glue to lid so that 10 mm/½″ of paper hangs free at each edge. Use scissors to clip out a small square of paper at each corner. Fold and glue the paper allowance onto the inside of lid.

6. Cut a piece of paper 2 mm/⅛″ smaller than lid and glue to inside of lid.

7. Using the same method described in step 5 cover liner pieces (C) with paper and glue in place inside box.

8. To make rolled paper knob, cut a strip of paper about 100 mm/4″ long and 20 mm/¾″ wide at one end, tapering to 10 mm/½″ wide at the other end. Cover wrong side of paper with glue. Roll it tightly, starting from the wider end and keeping coloured side out. Trim the strip when you have a knob of width you desire. Glue onto lid.

Note: Contrasting coloured papers look attractive, especially in this small box. We used a textured Japanese paper.

A round button with a shank could be used for a knob instead of rolled paper. Just make a slit in the centre of the lid, add a drop of craft glue, then insert the shank of the button.

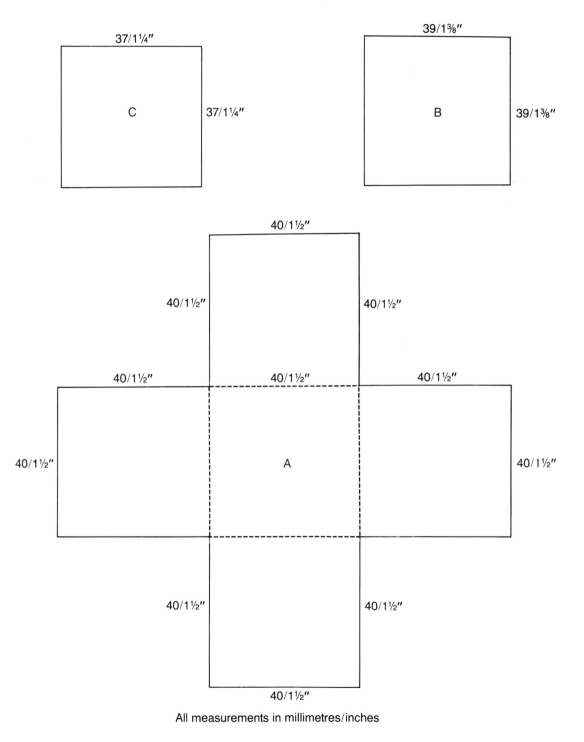

All measurements in millimetres/inches

COLLAGE BOX

The instructions given here are for the collage technique itself. The box pictured is a smaller version of the Rectangular Box on page 12. Make your box the size you desire; cover the base following the Rectangular Box instructions, then make the lid following the instructions below.

YOU WILL NEED:
heavy cardboard
paper (contrasting colours)
glue stick

1. Cut very small pieces of paper in geometric shapes: triangular, square etc. The shapes can be irregular and have any number of sides. Use the picture as a guide.

2. Cover one side of the lid with glue. Arrange the cut-paper pieces on the lid, butting edges together and overlapping some shapes until no cardboard is visible.

3. Cut four strips of paper, making each strip 20 mm/1″ wider than and as long as the lid sides. Glue the strips onto each lid edge so that 5 mm/¼″ of the strip forms a border on the collage side and gluing the remaining paper allowance to inside of lid.

4. Cut a piece of paper 10 mm/½″ larger on all sides than lid liner. Glue onto lid liner so that 10 mm/½″ of paper hangs free at each edge. Use scissors to clip out a small square of paper at each corner. Fold and glue the paper allowances to inside of liner. Glue the lid liner and the lid together, covered sides out, centering the liner piece on the lid.

BOX WITH CUT-OUT BOWS

YOU WILL NEED:
heavy cardboard
stiff plain-coloured paper
tissue paper to match
glue stick
clear-drying craft glue
sharp scalpel or small cutting knife

158/6¼"

A
55/2¼"

152/6"   49/2"   152/6"   49/2"

B
30/1¼"

All measurements in millimetres/inches

1. Cut A and B to measurements shown on diagrams. Cut two A pieces and one B piece from heavy cardboard. Score B along broken lines.

2. Cut one piece of paper the same size as A and one piece of paper the same size as B and glue in place on one side of one A piece (base) and the unscored side of B.

3. Cut a piece of paper 10 mm/½" larger on all sides than the A piece. Glue onto uncovered side of A so that 10 mm/½" of paper hangs free at each edge of A. Use scissors to clip out a small square of paper at each corner. Fold and glue the paper allowances to covered side of A.

4. Fold up B (box wall) and tape ends together where they meet to form a corner (tape on the outside). Cut a strip of paper 20 mm/1" wider and 20 mm/1" longer than B. Glue strip around B so that 10 mm/½" of paper hangs free at top and bottom edge of B. Overlap the excess 20 mm/1" of paper at the ends. Fold and glue paper allowances to the inside of wall.

5. Run a line of craft glue around the bottom edge of B. Carefully place B in the centre of the covered A base and hold for a few seconds until glue becomes sticky. Place a weight (e.g. a book) on top, check positioning, then allow to dry.

6. Cut a strip of paper 10 mm/½" wider on all sides than the remaining A piece (lid). Glue paper on lid so that 10 mm/½" hangs free at each edge of lid. Use scissors to clip out a small square of paper at each corner. Fold and glue the paper allowances to other side of lid. Cover the other side with a same-size piece of tissue paper (this will be the top of the box).

7. Cut another piece of paper the same size as A. Mark positions of bows on this paper with a light pencil dot. You can either draw the bow lines in with pencil or cut, using the picture as a guide. Practise on scrap paper first. Using a sharp scalpel or knife, cut along the bow lines, taking care not to cut out any pieces. Carefully lift the edges of the bow up with the scalpel point.

8. Apply stick glue over the side of lid covered in tissue paper and carefully position the cut-out paper on top of the box. Keep the bow edges free of glue.

BOX WITH CUT-OUT DAISIES

YOU WILL NEED:
heavy cardboard
stiff plain-coloured paper*
tissue paper to match
glue stick
sharp scalpel or small cutting knife

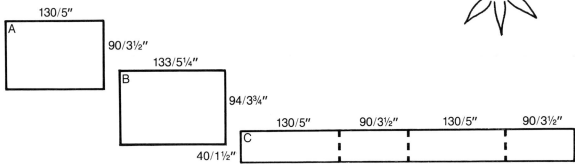

All measurements in millimetres/inches

* Tissue paper or stiff paper can be used to cover the bottom of box and the inside of lid. The box pictured has a tissue paper covering with the cut-out lid top covered in stiff paper.

1. Cut A, B and C to measurements shown on diagrams. Cut all pieces from heavy cardboard and score C along broken lines.

2. Cut a piece of paper the same size as A and glue in place on one side of A. Cut a piece of tissue paper the same size as B (lid) and glue in place on one side of B (lid top). Cut a piece of paper the same size as C and glue in place on the unscored side (inside) of C.

3. Fold C (walls) around A (base), covered sides in, and tape the edges of C and A together tightly at right angles to each other (it is easiest to do this by holding edges of C tightly against A one by one and taping each edge in place). Tape ends of C together where they meet to form a corner.

4. Cut a strip of paper 20 mm/1″ wider and 20 mm/1″ longer than C. Glue paper around C so that 10 mm/½″ of paper hangs free at top and bottom edge of C. Overlap the excess 20 mm/1″ of paper at the ends. At each corner of bottom paper allowance, use scissors to clip in to the edge of cardboard. Fold and glue paper allowances onto base and to inside of walls.

5. Hold B (lid) along one long edge of the box and place a tape hinge along the length of the edges where B and C meet (back of the box). Cut a piece of paper larger than the tape and glue it over tape to conceal hinge. Cut a piece of paper 10 mm/½″ larger on three sides than B. Glue onto B so that 10 mm/½″ of paper hangs free at each edge of B except at back of box, where paper sits flush. Use scissors to clip out a small square of paper at each corner. Fold and glue the paper allowances onto the top of lid.

6. Cut a piece of paper the same size as B. Mark the daisy design in light pencil or use the picture as a guide to cut it. Use the scalpel and cut each petal carefully – start from the tip of the petal and curve the knife to the flower centre; don't cut right through the centre. Practise on scrap paper first. Make a half moon cut to suggest the flower centre. Group a few daisies together; cut them various sizes.

7. Lift the tip of each petal with the scalpel point. Cover the tissue-covered side of B with glue and position the cut-out paper piece on the box top.

Note: To make gift cards like the one pictured, just cut a rectangular strip of paper, cut out the design following the instructions given in step 6 above and fold the card in half.

TORN TISSUE PAPER BOX

YOU WILL NEED:
heavy cardboard
tissue paper (3 or 4 colours)
spray glue or glue stick
tape

The box pictured is a smaller version of the Large Square Box on page 6. Make your box any size – just keep the base square (B) 2 mm/¼″ smaller than the lid (A) and size the wall lengths correspondingly. Follow steps 1 to 5 for the Large Square Box, covering with 2 or 3 layers of tissue paper, then add the tissue paper flower as described below.

6. Tear petal shapes of tissue paper along the grain of the paper. To find the grain, tear the paper one way, then the other; it will tear easily in one direction and this is along the grain. It is much easier to tear flower petals along the grain. Practise until you have a number of petals in various sizes and colours and arrange them into a flower shape. Use the picture as a guide. When you are satisfied with the flower, use a glue stick to glue the petals in place, positioning the darker colours first, then overlaying the lighter colours of tissue.

STATIONERY SET

YOU WILL NEED:
heavy cardboard
light cardboard
paper
tassel
5 cm/2″ cord or twisted thread
spray adhesive or glue stick
round pencil
elastic bands
notepaper

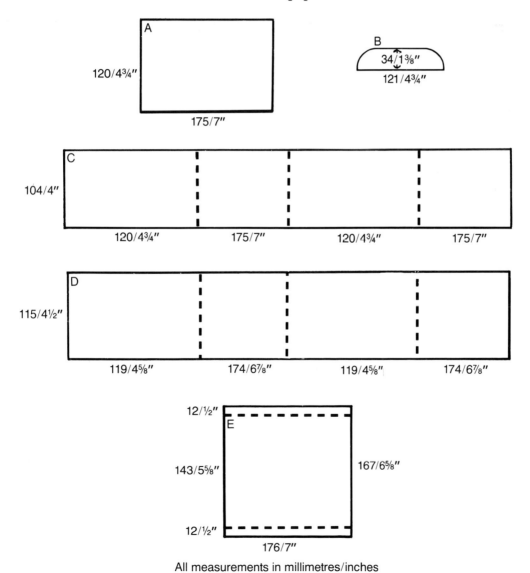

A

120/4¾″

175/7″

B

34/1⅜″

121/4¾″

C

104/4″

120/4¾″   175/7″   120/4¾″   175/7″

D

115/4½″

119/4⅝″   174/6⅞″   119/4⅝″   174/6⅞″

12/½″

E

143/5⅝″   167/6⅝″

12/½″

176/7″

All measurements in millimetres/inches

1. Cut A, B, C, D and E to measurements shown on diagrams. Cut A and B from heavy cardboard. Cut C, D and E from light cardboard, cutting the 176 mm/ 7″ length of E along the grain so that the piece will bend across the 167 mm/ 6⅝″ width. Score along broken lines.

2. Cut a piece of paper the same size as A and glue in place on one side of A (inside). Fold C (walls) around A (base), covered side in, and tape edges tightly together at right angles to each other (it is easiest to do this by holding edges of C tightly against A one by one and taping each edge in place). Tape ends of C together where they meet to form a corner, and reinforce on the inside also.

3. Check that D (box liner) fits neatly into box. If too large, trim to fit. Cut a strip of paper 30 mm/1½″ wider and as long as D. Glue to unscored side of D so that 20 mm/1″ hangs free at the top and 10 mm/½″ hangs free at the bottom of D. Fold and glue the paper allowances to other side of D. Fold D with covered side in and tape the ends where they meet to form a corner.

4. Cut a strip of paper 20 mm/1″ wider and 20 mm/1″ longer than the circumference of C. Glue around C so that 10 mm/½″ of paper hangs free at top and bottom edge of C. At each corner of bottom paper allowance, use scissors to clip the paper up to edge of cardboard. Fold and glue the allowances onto the base and to the inside of walls. Cut a piece of paper the same size as base and glue on base.

5. Place a length of tape along one 167 mm/6⅝″ edge of E (lid) allowing half the width of the tape to hang free from the edge. Use scissors to clip V-shapes out of the tape every 10 mm/½″. Starting at one end of the curved edge of one B piece (lid end), tape the B piece and E together by bending E to fit around the curve of B and holding the edges tightly together at right angles before securing with tape. Repeat for the other lid end.

If the lid is too flexible and does not hold the correct shape, the ends can be reinforced by cutting two more lid-end pieces and taping them on the outside of the existing ends.

6. To cover the lid, cut a piece of paper about 10 mm/½″ larger on all sides than the lid. Glue it onto the lid so that 10 mm/½″ hangs free at each edge. Glue the paper allowance at the front and back of the lid onto the inside. Use scissors to clip V-shapes from the paper allowances at each end and glue them onto the lid ends. Cut two pieces of paper the same size as lid ends, but with 10 mm/½″ extra on the straight edge. Glue in place onto each end and glue the 10 mm/½″ paper allowance inside the ends. Cut two more pieces of paper the same size as lid ends and glue to the inside of the lid ends.

7. Place the lid and the back edge of the box together. Place a piece of tape along the inside of one long edge of the lid and one long edge of the box so that it forms a hinge.

8. Using a skewer or large needle, pierce a hole through the front edge of the lid. Thread the loop of a tassel through the hole and tape the loop to the inside of the lid. Cut a piece of paper to fit into the inside of the lid, plus 30 mm/ 1½″ extra on the back edge to cover the hinge. Glue the paper inside the lid, gluing the extra 30 mm/1½″ onto the inside back edge of the box.

9. Glue the liner in place inside the box.

10. Cut strips of paper and glue them onto notepaper to make a matching set. Cut a strip of paper as long as the pencil and 5 mm/¼″ wider. Tape a cord or twisted thread loop onto the end of the pencil. Glue paper cover around the pencil. Hold the paper with elastic bands until the glue dries. Cut a narrow strip paper and glue it around the end of the pencil.

DESK SET

YOU WILL NEED:
heavy cardboard
light cardboard
cardboard cylinder
paper
spray adhesive or glue stick
craft glue

A, B, C, D, E, F, G and H should be cut to measurements shown on diagrams.

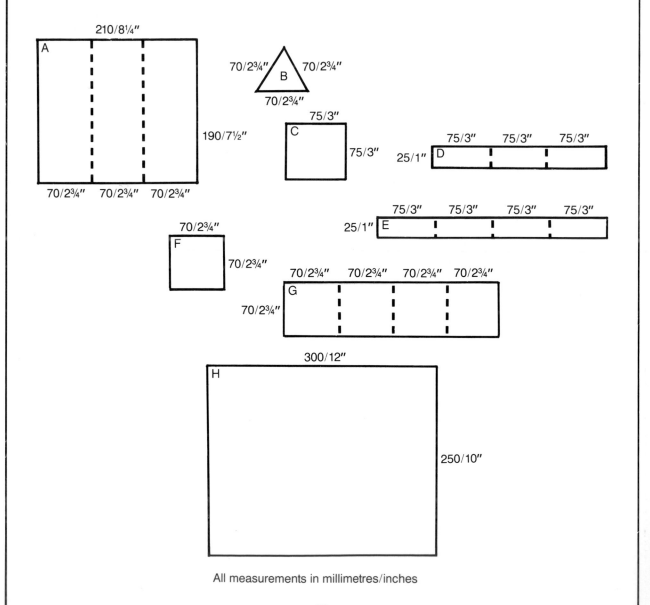

All measurements in millimetres/inches

TRIANGULAR BRUSH HOLDER

1. Cut A (wall) from light cardboard and B (base) from heavy cardboard. Score A along broken lines. Cut a piece of paper the same size as A and glue in place on the unscored side of A. Cut a piece of paper the same size as B and glue in place on one side of B.

2. Fold A into a triangular shape, covered side in. Fold around B, covered side in, and tape the edges of B and A tightly together at right angles to each other (it is easiest to do this by holding edges of B tightly against A one by one and taping each edge in place). Tape along the length where the ends of A meet to form a corner.

3. Cut a piece of paper 10 mm/½″ larger on all sides than A. Glue around A so that 10 mm/½″ of paper hangs free at top and bottom edge. Overlap the excess 20 mm/1″ of paper at the ends. At each corner of bottom allowance, use scissors to clip paper in to the edge of the cardboard. Fold and glue allowances to inside of triangle and onto base.

PENCIL HOLDER

1. Cut F (base) from heavy cardboard and G (walls) from light cardboard. Score along broken lines.

2. Cut a piece of paper the same size as F and glue in place on one side of F. Cut a piece of paper the same size as G and glue in place on the unscored side of G.

3. Fold G along scored lines. Fold G around F, covered sides in, and tape the edges of G and F tightly together at right angles to each other (it is easiest to do this by holding edges of G tightly against F one by one and taping each edge in place). Tape ends of G together where they meet to form a corner.

4. Cut a strip of paper 20 mm/1″ wider and 10 mm/½″ longer than G. Glue it around G, leaving 10 mm/½″ free at both top and bottom edge, and overlapping the paper where the ends meet.
At each corner of bottom allowance, use scissors to clip the paper in to the edge of cardboard. Fold and glue the allowances onto the base and to the inside of walls. Smooth out any wrinkles in the paper.

DOUBLE PAPER CLIP TRAY

1. Cut two C pieces from heavy cardboard and one D and E (walls) from light cardboard. Score D and E along broken lines.

2. Cut 2 pieces of paper the same size as C and glue in place on one side of each C piece (inside of each tray base).

3. Cut 2 pieces of paper the same size as D. Use one piece to cover unscored

side of three 75 mm/3″ sections of E (inside). Glue the other in place on unscored side of D (walls).

4. Fold E around one C piece, covered sides in, and tape edges of E and C tightly together at right angles to each other (it is easiest to do this by holding edges of E tightly against C one by one and taping each edge in place). Tape ends of E together where they meet to form a corner.

5. Use similar method to above to tape D to the remaining C piece, covered sides in.

6. Tape the two 'trays' together, placing the uncovered side of E between the trays and using tape on the base and the outside of walls.

7. Cut a piece of paper large enough to cover both sides of the uncovered E section; glue it in position.

8. Cut a strip of paper 20 mm/1″ wider than the walls and 10 mm/½″ longer than the circumference of the walls. Glue it around the tray so that 10 mm/½″ of paper hangs free at the top and bottom edge and the 10 mm/½″ at ends overlaps. At each corner of bottom allowance and at the centre division, use scissors to clip in to the edge of cardboard. Fold and glue the paper allowances onto the inside of tray and onto base.

ROUND PENCIL HOLDER

1. Cut the cylinder to the length you desire. Cut a circle from light cardboard that will fit inside one end of the cylinder.

2. Cut a piece of paper the same length and the width of the circumference of cylinder and glue inside the cylinder.
Cut a piece of paper 20 mm/1″ wider than the circumference of cylinder and 20 mm/1″ longer than cylinder. Glue it around cylinder so that 10 mm/½″ of paper hangs free at top and bottom edge. Overlap the excess 20 mm/1″ of paper at the ends. Fold and glue the paper allowances to the inside of cylinder.

3. Cut a piece of paper the same size as circle and glue in place on one side of circle. Fit it into one end of the cylinder, covered side inside, and glue in place using craft glue.

TO ASSEMBLE DESK SET

1. Cut H (base) from heavy cardboard. Cut a piece of paper 10 mm/½″ larger on all sides than H. Glue onto H so that 10 mm/½″ of paper hangs free at each edge of H. Use scissors to clip out a small square of paper at each corner. Fold and glue the paper allowances to other side of H.

2. Glue all components of the set onto the base in the position you desire using craft glue.

FABRIC BOXES

EASY HAT BOX

YOU WILL NEED:
heavy cardboard
light cardboard
spray adhesive or glue stick
lightweight fabric
braid
ribbon

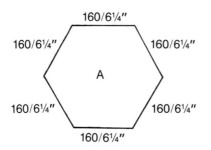

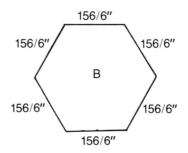

160/6¼"	160/6¼"	160/6¼"	160/6¼"	160/6¼"	160/6¼"

C

45/1¾"

156/6"	156/6"	156/6"	156/6"	156/6"	156/6"

D

150/6"

All measurements in millimetres/inches

1. Cut A, B, C and D to measurements shown on diagrams. (See instructions on page 3 on how to draw a hexagon for cutting out A and B.) Cut A and B from heavy cardboard and C and D from light cardboard. Score along broken lines.

2. Glue cardboard pieces to the wrong side of the fabric, with unscored sides of cardboard pieces facing fabric. Trim fabric flush with the edges of the cardboard (covered side will be inside of the box).

3. Fold C (lid rim) around A (lid), covered sides in, and tape the edges of C and A together tightly at right angles to each other (it is easiest to do this by holding edges of C tightly against A one by one and taping each piece in place). Tape ends of C together where they meet to form a corner.

4. Use the same method as above to attach D (walls) to B (base).

5. Cut a strip of fabric 40 mm/2″ wider than D and 20 mm/1″ longer than the circumference of D. Glue fabric around D so that 20 mm/1″ of fabric hangs free at top and bottom edges and the ends of the fabric strip overlap neatly. At each corner of bottom allowance, use scissors to clip fabric in to the edge of the cardboard. Fold and glue the fabric allowances inside the box and onto the base.

6. Cut a hexagon of fabric 20 mm/1″ larger on all sides than A. Glue it onto lid so that 20 mm/1″ of fabric hangs free on each side. At each corner, use scissors to clip fabric in to the edge of the cardboard. Glue the allowance onto lid rim.

7. Cut a strip of fabric 20 mm/1″ wider than C and 20 mm/1″ longer than the circumference of C. Glue the fabric strip around the rim, aligning one raw edge with the edge of lid top and rim and overlapping the ends of the fabric strip where they meet. Fold and glue the 20 mm/1″ allowance onto the inside of lid rim.

8. Glue ribbon and braid around box and then glue a ribbon bow as you desire.

9. Cut a hexagon of fabric slightly smaller than B and glue to underside of base.

SET OF TRIANGULAR BOXES

YOU WILL NEED:
heavy cardboard
light cardboard
very light cardboard
lightweight fabric (two colours)
spray adhesive or glue stick

Cut all shapes to measurements shown on diagrams.

1. Cut A (large box base) and C (large box lid) from heavy cardboard. Cut B (wall) and D (lid rim) from light cardboard. Score along broken lines. Cut E (box liner) and F (lid liner) from very light cardboard.

2. Cut a triangle of fabric the same size as A and glue it to one side of A (inside).

3. Fold B around A, covered side in, and tape the edges of B and A together tightly at right angles to each other (it is easiest to do this by holding edges of B tightly against A one by one and taping each edge in place). Tape ends of B together where they meet to form a corner.

4. Cut a strip of fabric 20 mm/1″ wider than B and 20 mm/1″ longer than the circumference of B. Glue around B so that 10 mm/½″ of fabric hangs free at top and bottom edge of B and ends overlap neatly. At each corner of bottom allowance, use scissors to clip in to the edge of the cardboard. Fold over allowances and trim any excess fabric. Glue to the inside of box and onto base.

5. Fold E along scored lines and tape ends together where they meet to form a corner. Use same method as above to cover unscored side of E and glue in place inside box.

6. Cut a fabric triangle the same size as lid and glue it to one side of lid (inside). Construct the box lid in the same way as the box.
Cut a piece of wadding the same size as lid and glue it to the top of lid. Cut a triangle of fabric large enough to cover the lid top and walls plus a 10 mm/½″ allowance on all sides. Use spray adhesive to cover the lid with fabric so that 10 mm/½″ of fabric hangs free at each edge. Fold the fabric in at each corner and glue it neatly so the fold runs along the corner edge of the lid rim. Fold the 10 mm/½″ allowance inside the lid and trim it; glue in place.
Assemble and cover the lid liner in the same way as the box liner and glue inside lid rim.

7. Cut four pieces each of G, H, I, J, K and L and construct small boxes (pieces G, H and K) and small box lids (pieces I, J and L) using the same method as described for the large box.

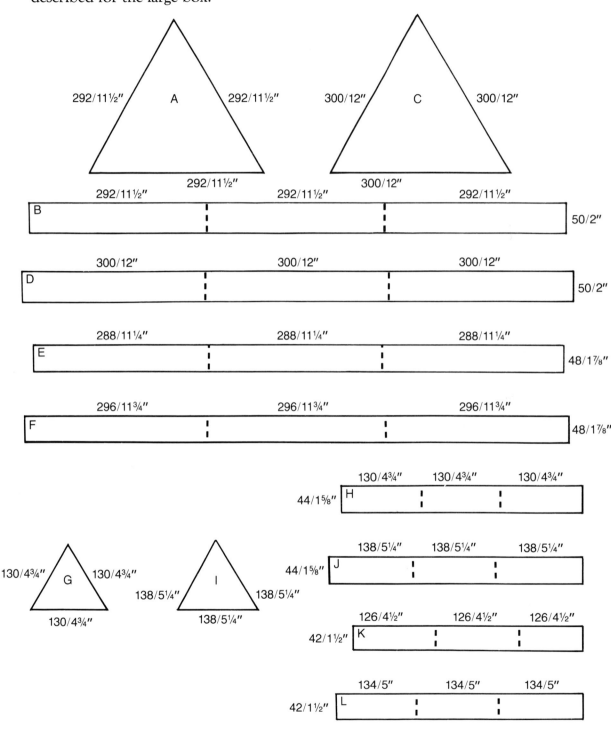

All measurements in millimetres/inches

PADDED HAT BOXES

<small>You will need:</small>
heavy cardboard
light cardboard
lightweight fabric
thin wadding
spray adhesive or glue stick
ribbon (optional)

A
Lid

235/9¼″ (313/12¼″) diameter

B
Base

227/8¾″ (305/11¾″) diameter

C
Lid liner

231/9″ (309/12″) diameter

D
Base
liner

225/8⅝″ (303/11⅝″) diameter

E
Under base
cover

225/8⅝″ (303/11⅝″) diameter

F   780/31″ (1040/41″)
42/1¾″

G   780/31″ (1040/41″)
39/1½″

750/29½″ (1000/39½″)
H
150/6″

750/29½″ (1000/39½″)
I
146/5¾″

Large hat box measurements in brackets

All measurements in millimetres/inches

1. Cut all shapes to measurements shown on diagrams. Cut A and B from heavy cardboard. Cut C, D, E, two pieces of F, G, H and I from light cardboard.

2. Attach a strip of tape along one long edge of one F piece (lid rim), allowing half the width of the tape to hang free from the edge. Use scissors to clip V-shapes from the tape every 15 mm/½″. Hold A next to the edge of F that has tape attached so that adhesive side of tapes faces in towards circle. Keeping the edges of each piece tightly together at right angles, press the first piece of tape onto A. Roll the card strip around the circle, pressing each piece of tape across onto the circle so the strip sits flush with the circle edge. When ends of the strip meet, trim so they overlap about 10 mm/½″ and tape together firmly.
(See figures 1-3)

Figure 1: Tape along lid rim; clip tape

Figure 2: Attach rim to lid

Figure 3: Overlap ends and tape together

3. Use same method as above to attach H (box wall) to B (base). (See figure 10).

4. Cut a piece of wadding about the same size as A. Glue wadding to the lid top and trim the wadding edges flush with lid edge. Cut a circle of fabric 20 mm/¾″ larger all around than A. Glue it over the wadding so that 20 mm/¾″ allowance hangs free all around. Use scissors to clip V-shapes from the allowance every 10 mm/½″. Glue the allowance onto the rim, pulling fabric firmly across the rim. (See figures 4-5)

Figure 4: Glue wadding to lid, and trim

Figure 5: Cover lid with fabric

5. Cut a strip of fabric 20 mm/¾″ larger all around than the remaining F piece (lid rim cover). Glue to F so that 20 mm/¾″ of fabric hangs free at each edge of F. Fold the 20 mm/¾″ allowance over and glue to other side of F on one long edge only. (See figure 6)

6. Apply glue to the lid rim and the uncovered side of the F strip. Glue F strip to the rim, so that the edge of F covered with folded fabric sits flush with top edge of the lid. Trim ends of F so that they meet without overlapping and glue the fabric allowance across ends so that the join is concealed. Fold and glue the bottom edge allowance to the inside of lid rim so that it covers both F edges. (See figure 6)

7. Cut a strip of fabric 20 mm/¾″ larger all around than G (lid rim liner). Glue fabric to G so that 20 mm/¾″ of fabric hangs free at each edge. Fold and glue allowance over to the other side of G on two long and one short ends. Glue the rim liner onto the inside of lid rim, covered side visible, trimming the ends of the strip (don't cut fabric allowance) so they meet without overlapping. Glue the unfolded fabric allowance over the join to conceal it. Hold the lid rim in place with pegs until the glue is dry. (See figure 7)

Figure 6: Glue lid rim cover to lid rim   Figure 7: Glue lid rim liner inside lid rim

8. Cut a piece of wadding about the same size as C (lid liner). Glue wadding to lid liner and trim the wadding edges flush with C edge. Cut a circle of fabric 20 mm/¾″ larger all around than C. Glue over wadding so that 20 mm/¾″ of fabric hangs free all around edge of C. Use scissors to clip V-shapes from allowance every 10 mm/½″ and glue onto the other side of C. Glue uncovered side of C onto the inside of the lid. (See figures 8 and 9)

Figure 8: Cover lid liner with fabric Figure 9: Glue lid liner inside lid Figure 10: Construct box as for lid

9. Cut a strip of fabric 20 mm/¾″ wider than H and 20 mm/1″ longer than the circumference of H. Glue to H so that 10 mm/½″ of fabric hangs free at top and bottom edges and ends overlap neatly. Fold and glue the top allowance inside the box. Use scissors to clip V-shapes from bottom allowance every 10 mm/½″ and glue allowance onto the base. (See figures 11, 12 and 13)

Figure 11: Cover walls with fabric Figure 12: Clip fabric allowance at base Figure 13: Glue allowance to base

10. Fit I (box liner) into the box. Remove and trim ends so they meet without overlapping. Cut a strip of fabric 20 mm/¾″ larger on all sides than I. Glue to I so that 20 mm/¾″ of fabric hangs free at each edge. Fold and glue allowance over to the other side of I on two long and one short ends. Glue liner into box, covered side visible, gluing the unfolded fabric allowance over the join to conceal it.

11. Pad and cover D (base liner) using the same method as described for C (lid liner). Glue D into box.

12. Using method described above, cover E (under-base cover) with fabric only and glue to the underside of base.

Note: Boxes can be tied with ribbon as pictured, or attach a cord as for Oval Box (page 9), before lining the box.

PATCHWORK SEWING BOX

YOU WILL NEED:
heavy cardboard
light cardboard
lightweight fabric (six different prints)
spray adhesive or glue stick
book binding tape or packaging tape
cord or twisted thread
2 metal rings
thread
quilting thread
thin wadding

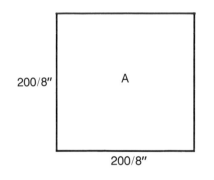

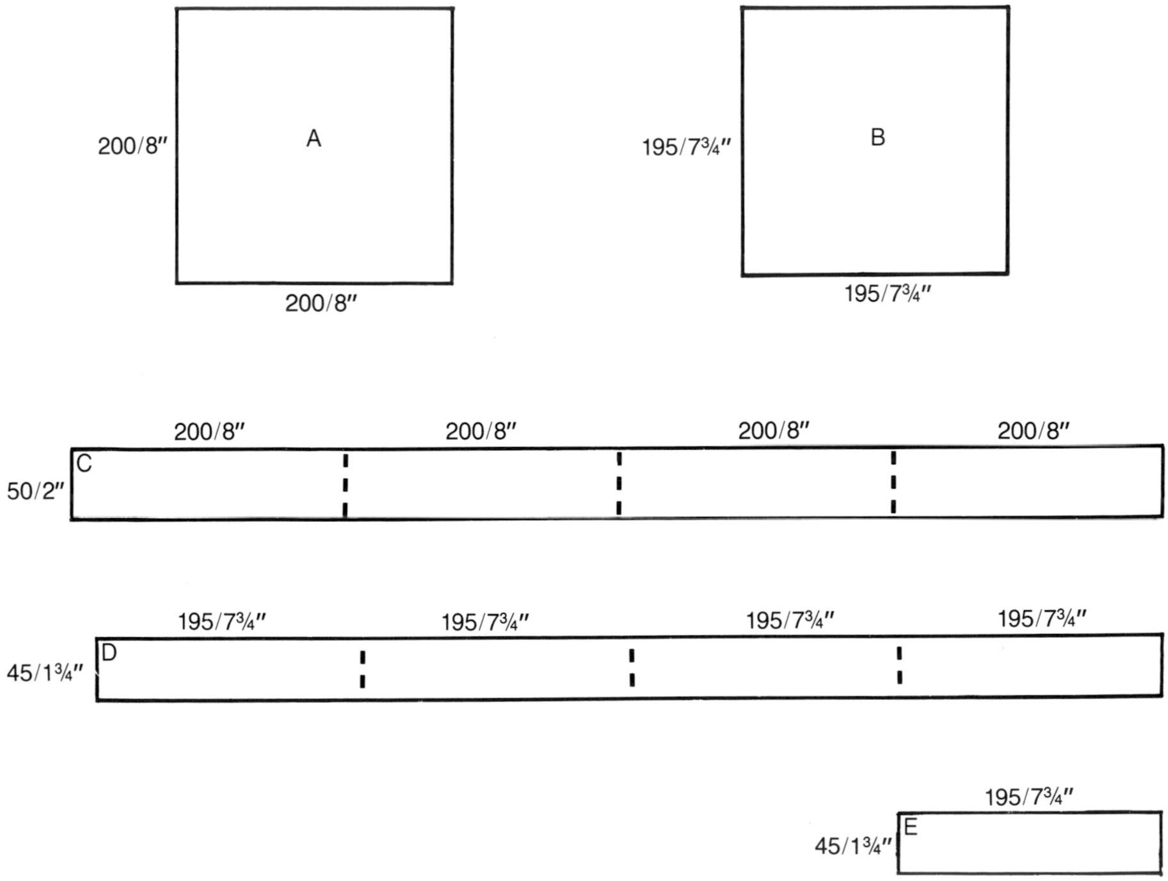

200/8″
A
200/8″
195/7¾″
B
195/7¾″
200/8″
200/8″
200/8″
200/8″
C
50/2″
195/7¾″
195/7¾″
195/7¾″
195/7¾″
D
45/1¾″
195/7¾″
E
45/1¾″

All measurements in millimetres/inches

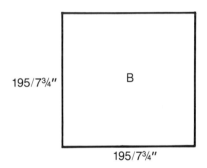

This box looks very attractive if the liners and box divider are made up in the same fabric, contrasting the borders, as in our picture.

1. Cut A, B, C, D and E to measurements shown on diagrams. Cut two A pieces (lid and base) from heavy cardboard. Cut two B pieces (liners) and C, D and E from light cardboard.

2. Cut strips of fabric 25 mm/1″ wide, along the grain of the fabric. Cut a square of fabric (for patchwork centre) 60 x 60 mm/2½ x 2½″.

3. Make lid cover by stitching one fabric strip along one edge of the fabric square (right sides together), allowing a 5 mm/¼″ seam. Trim the end of the strip so that it is level with the edge of the square. Press the strip open.

4. Working in a clockwise direction, stitch another fabric strip so that it extends across the narrow end of the first strip and along the side of the square (keep right sides together). Trim the end of the strip so that it is level with the edge of the square. Press the strip open. Continue attaching and pressing the strips in a clockwise direction until there are five strips on each side of the square. Dark and light strips can be used on opposite sides of the square as pictured on our box, if desired.

5. Cut a piece of wadding and a piece of backing fabric the same size as the patchwork piece and tack onto the wrong side of the patchwork piece. Tack the three layers together in a grid of tacking lines to secure the layers.

6. Stitch a line of quilting next to each seam on each strip, using quilting thread and running stitches.

7. Trim the wadding and backing fabric flush with the patchwork piece.

8. Cut border strips of fabric 30 mm/1½″ wide and stitch around the square.

9. To make the box wall cover, cut a total of seventeen 60 x 60 mm/2½ x 2½″ squares from the fabrics. Stitch the squares together in a strip (allowing 5 mm/¼″ seams), alternating the prints as pictured. Press seams flat.

10. Cut border strips of fabric 20 mm/1″ wide and stitch borders along the long edges of the patchwork strip. Press seams flat.

11. Glue the patchwork square (lid cover) to one A piece. Fold and glue excess fabric to the other side of A.

12. Fold C (wall) around remaining A piece (base) and tape the edges of C and A together tightly at right angles to each other (it is easiest to do this by holding edges of C tightly against A one by one and taping each edge in place). Tape ends of C where they meet to form a corner.

13. Cut a strip of wadding the same size as C and glue around the outside of C. Glue the patchwork strip around C, overlapping ends of strip neatly and gluing in place. (Where the ends meet will be the back of the box.) Fold and glue the borders at top and bottom to the inside of the box and onto the base.

14. Place the lid against the back wall of the box (where patchwork strip joins) and tape the two pieces together on the inside along their length, forming a hinge. Glue a strip of fabric over the tape to conceal it.

15. Cut a piece of fabric 20 mm/1″ larger on all sides than B. Glue to one B piece (lid liner) so that 20 mm/1″ hangs free at each edge. Use scissors to clip out a small square of fabric at each corner. Fold and glue the fabric allowances to the other side of B.
Tape cord threaded with two metal rings to the centre front edge of the lid. Glue liner to the inside of the lid.

16. Cut a piece of wadding the same size as B and glue to the remaining B piece (base liner). Use method described in step 15 to cover liner with fabric. Glue liner inside the box.

17. Cut a piece of wadding the same size as D (wall liner) and glue to the unscored side of D. Use method described in step 15 to cover wadded side of D with fabric. Fold liner up, covered side inwards, and fit in place, gluing if necessary.

18. Cover both sides of E (divider) with one piece of fabric, folding fabric around so that one long edge is covered. Cut fabric flush with the edges of E on remaining long side and the two short sides. Place divider into box so that folded edge is at top as pictured; glue if necessary.

PINCUSHION BOX

YOU WILL NEED:
heavy cardboard
light cardboard
lightweight fabric (two prints)
felt scrap
fibre filling
cord or twisted thread
metal ring

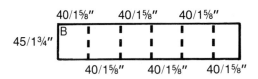

1. Cut A using tracing of actual-size hexagonal shape provided and B to measurements shown on diagram. Cut two A pieces from heavy cardboard. Cut B from light cardboard. Score B along broken lines.

2. Fold B (walls) around one A piece (base) and tape the edges of B and A together tightly at right angles to each other (it is easiest to do this by holding edges of B tightly against A one by one and taping each edge in place). Tape ends of B together where they meet to form a corner.

3. Cut a strip of fabric 30 mm/1½″ wider than B and 10 mm/½″ longer than the circumference of B. Glue fabric around B so that 20 mm/1″ of fabric hangs free at top edge and 10 mm/½″ hangs free at bottom edge, and ends overlap neatly. Fold and glue fabric allowance to inside of box and onto base.

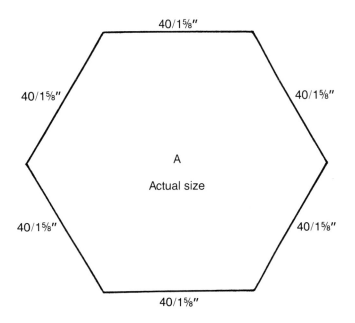

All measurements in millimetres/inches

4. Cut a piece of fabric 10 mm/½″ larger on all sides than A. Glue to remaining A piece (lid) so that 10 mm/½″ of fabric hangs free at each edge. At each corner, use scissors to clip fabric in to edge of the cardboard. Fold and glue the fabric allowances to inside of lid.

5. Hold lid, covered side out, at right angles to box along one side and tape along this one side only, to form a hinge. Cut a piece of fabric larger than the tape and glue it over the tape to conceal the hinge.

6. Tape a loop of cord threaded with a metal ring to the front edge of the lid. Cut a hexagon of felt slightly smaller than the lid. Glue this needle holder to the inside of the lid.

7. Cut a circle of fabric large enough to hold the wadding for the pincushion. Place a ball of fibre filling in the centre of the wrong side of the fabric circle. Gather up the edges of the fabric and tie it into a ball with thread or an elastic band. Glue the pincushion ball onto the inside of the box base.

LOVELY LACQUERED BOXES:
ROUND AND SQUARE

ROUND BOX

Make the box following the directions for the Round Box on page 7. Make the box (B) 5 mm/¼″ smaller than the lid (A). Cover the box with fabric instead of paper. (We also lined this box with fabric.)

Coat the box with two or three thin coats of varnish, allowing varnish to dry in between coats. Lightly sand the box with fine sandpaper. Wipe any powdery residue off the box with a cloth and apply more coats of varnish, sanding between every two or three coats.

Apply enough varnish to build up the finish you desire, taking care not to apply so much that the lid no longer fits. If you wish to build up a very thick layer of varnish, make the lid larger.

SQUARE BOX

This box is covered with a preprinted craft fabric panel and lined in a contrasting fabric. The size of your box will depend on the fabric panel you choose. So cut the box lid according to the panel size. You can follow one of the basic box styles in this book to construct your box. Try the Box with Cut-Out Daisies on page 23.

The box can be lined with fabric-covered pieces, cut slightly smaller than the box pieces. See the instructions for making fabric liners for the Patchwork Sewing Box on page 40.

Make a lid lifter with a bead-threaded loop of cord and glue it to the front edge of the lid, between the lid and its lining.

To finish the box, apply varnish using the same method as for the Round Box. Keep lid open while varnish is drying by placing a paint brush or pencil under the box lid.

CUTWORK BOX

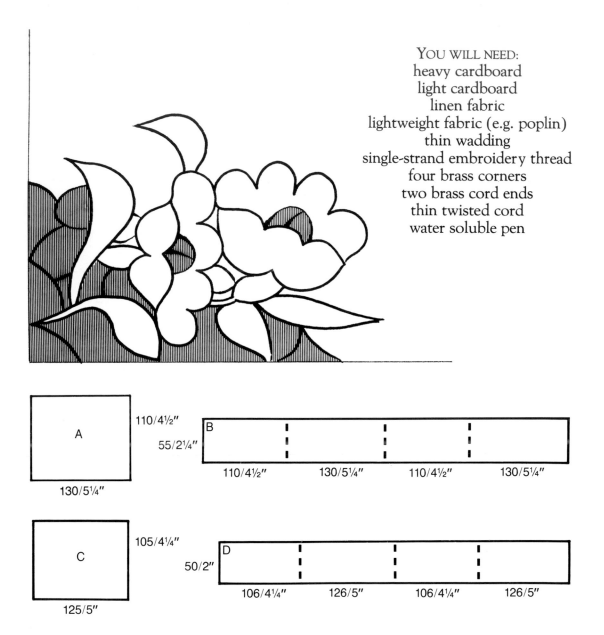

YOU WILL NEED:
heavy cardboard
light cardboard
linen fabric
lightweight fabric (e.g. poplin)
thin wadding
single-strand embroidery thread
four brass corners
two brass cord ends
thin twisted cord
water soluble pen

All measurements in millimetres/inches

1. Cut A, B, C and D to measurements shown on diagrams. Cut two A pieces from heavy cardboard. Cut B, two C pieces and D from light cardboard. Score along broken lines.

2. Cut a rectangle of linen 10 mm/½″ larger on all sides than A. Use a water soluble pen to transfer the cutwork design onto the left side, positioning it 30 mm/ 1¼″ from the fabric edge as shown in the picture.

3. Work very small running stitches along the solid lines. Stitch small, close buttonhole stitches over the running stitch lines, placing the ridge of the stitch on the side that is to be cut away. The cut-away areas are shaded on the design. Where a line has cut-away parts on both sides of it, work a bar of several long floating stitches over the line. Embroider the buttonhole stitch over the bar, without stitching through the fabric.

4. When design is complete, cut away the fabric in the shaded areas of the design.

5. Cut a piece of lightweight fabric the same size as A and glue in place on one A piece (lid). Glue the embroidered linen piece over the same side, so that 10 mm/½″ of fabric hangs free at each edge of A. Use scissors to clip out a small square of paper at each corner. Fold and glue the fabric allowance to the underside of lid. Glue or press brass corners onto the lid.

6. Fold B (walls) around the remaining A piece (base) and tape the edges of B and A together tightly at right angles to each other (it is easiest to do this by holding edges of B tightly against A one by one and taping each edge in place). Tape ends of B together where they meet to form a corner.

7. Cut a piece of linen 20 mm/1″ wider than B and 20 mm/1″ longer than the circumference of B. Glue to B so that 10 mm/½″ of fabric hangs free at top and bottom edge and ends overlap neatly. At each corner of bottom fabric allowance, use scissors to clip fabric in to edge of cardboard. Fold and glue the fabric allowances to the inside of box and onto the base.

8. Hold the lid at right angles to back wall of box and tape along this one side only, to form a hinge. Cut a lightweight piece of fabric larger than the tape and glue it over the tape to conceal the hinge. Tape brass cord ends threaded onto cord at centre front edge of box.

9. Cut two pieces of wadding the same size as C, and one the same size as D. Glue wadding to C pieces (lid and base liner) and to the unscored side of D (wall liner).

10. Cut two lightweight pieces of fabric 20 mm/1″ larger on all sides than C pieces. Cover the padded side of both C pieces using the same method described in step 7. Glue one liner to the inside of box base and one to the inside of lid.

11. Cut a strip of lightweight fabric 20 mm/1″ wider and 20 mm/1″ longer than D. Cover the padded side of D using the same method described in step 7. Fold and glue to inside of box walls.

12. Cut a piece of lightweight fabric slightly smaller than the box base and glue to underside of base.

BOX WITH PLEATED LID

YOU WILL NEED:
one sturdy shoe box
heavy cardboard
fabric
fusible interfacing
cord
braid
wadding
spray adhesive or glue stick

1. Cut the edges from the lid of shoe box and trim 3 mm/⅛" off from all sides.

2. Cut a strip of fabric 60 mm/2½" wider and twice as long as the lid. Fold fabric up into small pleats of about 7 mm/¼", every 15 mm/½" across the width of the fabric. Pin at the edge of the fabric to hold pleats in place.

3. Cut a piece of fusible interfacing the same size as pleated fabric. Press the interfacing onto the back of the fabric to hold pleats in place.

4. Trim pleated fabric so that it is 20 mm/1" larger on all sides than the lid. Glue it onto the lid so that there is an excess of 20 mm/1" of fabric at each edge. Trim the fabric at the corners to allow you to fold and glue the allowances to the other side of lid neatly.

5. Make a 10 mm/½" slit in the centre of the lid. Wrap each end of a cord length in tape. Insert the ends through the slit. Adjust height of the loop and trim ends. Tape them onto the back of the lid.

6. Cut a thick piece of cardboard the same size as the lid (will be lid liner). Cut a piece of fabric 10 mm/½" larger on all sides than lid liner. Glue to lid liner so that 10 mm/½" of fabric hangs free at each edge. Use scissors to clip out a small square of fabric at each corner. Fold and glue fabric allowances to the other side of liner. Glue liner inside lid.

7. Cut out a strip of wadding to cover the walls of the box. Trim edges flush with box. Cut a strip of fabric 40 mm/2" wider than box walls and 20 mm/ 1" longer than the circumference of box. Glue around box walls over wadding so that 20 mm/1" hangs free at top and bottom edge and ends overlap neatly. At each corner of bottom fabric allowance, use scissors to clip in to edge of cardboard. Fold and glue allowances to inside of box and onto the base.

8. Cut a piece of cardboard the same size as the box base (will be base liner). Cut a piece of wadding to cover one side of cardboard. Glue wadding to cardboard and trim flush with edges. Cut a piece of fabric 10 mm/½″ larger on all sides than base liner and cover using same method as described in step 6. Glue liner to inside of box base.

9. Cut cardboard pieces 5 mm/¼″ smaller than the walls and cover each in fabric as above. Glue the wall liners into the box.

10. Cut a piece of fabric slightly smaller than the base and glue it to the underside of base.

GATHERED AND PADDED JEWELLERY BOX

YOU WILL NEED:
heavy cardboard
light cardboard
fabric
wadding
tassel
16 cm x 9 cm/6½″ x 3½″ mirror
10 cm/½″ length of ribbon
craft glue

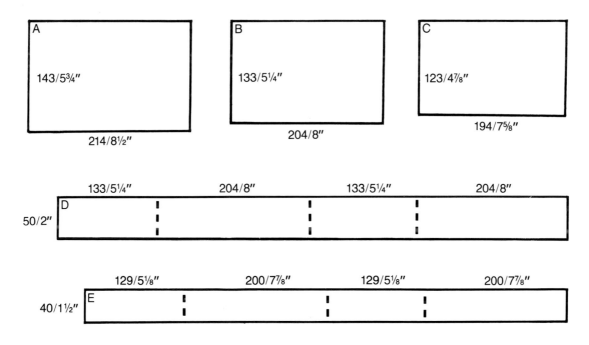

All measurements in millimetres/inches

1. Cut A, B, C, D and E to measurements shown in diagrams. Cut A, two B pieces, C and D from heavy cardboard. Cut E from light cardboard. Score along broken lines.

2. Cut a strip of fabric 9 cm/3½″ wide and 115 cm/45″ long. Run gathering threads 1 cm/½″ from the top and bottom edge of strip along the long edges. Gather up to measure 47.5 cm/18½″ and tie threads to hold in place.

3. Place D (box walls), scored side down, on wrong side of gathered fabric strip. Fabric strip should cover two 133 mm/5¼″ sides and one 204 mm/8″ side of D, with allowances. Fold and glue allowances of gathered strip to other side of D.

4. Cut a strip of fabric to cover remaining 204 mm/8″ side of D, adding a 20 mm/1″ allowance. Glue strip in position and fold and glue allowance to other side of D.

5. Cut a piece of wadding the same size as B and glue into place on one side of B (base). Cut a piece of fabric 10 mm/½″ larger on all sides than B and glue over wadding so that 10 mm/½″ of fabric hangs free at each edge. Fold and glue fabric allowances to other side.

6. Fold D, gathered side out, to make box walls and glue ends where they meet to form a corner. Trim any gathering thread visible on the outside of the box. Run a line of craft glue around the bottom edge of the box walls. Fit the base, padded side up, into the walls. Allow glue to dry.

7. Cut a piece of wadding the same size as A (lid) and glue in place on one side of A. Cut a piece of fabric 20 mm/1″ larger on all sides than A and glue over wadding so that 20 mm/1″ of fabric hangs free at each edge. Use scissors to clip out a small square of fabric at each corner. Fold and glue fabric allowances to other side.

8. Cut a 130 mm x 60 mm/5″ x 2¼″ hole from the centre of C (mirror frame). Cut a piece of wadding the same size as C and glue to C, cutting out centre frame hole and trimming edges flush with cardboard. Cut a piece of fabric 20 mm/1″ larger on all sides than frame. Glue fabric over wadding. Use scissors to clip the fabric in to the inside corners of the frame. Fold all fabric allowances to other side of frame, trim off any excess and glue allowances in place.

9. Hold lid, covered side out, at right angles to box along one side (back wall) and tape along this one side only, to form a hinge. Check positioning of lid to ensure it sits on the box correctly. Cut a piece of fabric larger than the tape and glue it over the tape to conceal the hinge.

10. Tape the piece of ribbon at the left back corner; one end on the back edge of lid and the other end on the left back box wall (see picture).

11. Glue a mirror to the back of the frame. Hold it in place with pegs and allow glue to dry. Tape the loop of a tassel to the top front edge of the frame, allowing enough length so tassel remains outside the box when the lid is closed. Glue the framed mirror to the underside of the lid.

12. Cut a strip of fabric 20 mm/1″ wider and 20 mm/1″ longer than E (box wall liner). Glue fabric to unscored side of E so that 10 mm/½″ of fabric hangs free at top and bottom edge and either end. Fold and glue fabric allowance onto other side of E and glue liner into place inside walls of box.
Cover the remaining B piece (base cover) as above and glue to the underside of base.

BEADED RING BOX

YOU WILL NEED:
cardboard cylinder
light cardboard
Thai silk
wadding scrap
bugle beads (long)
seed beads (round)
glue stick or spray adhesive
craft glue

1. Cut a 35 mm/1½″ long section of cylinder. Cut a circle (base) from light cardboard that will fit inside one end of the cylinder. Cut a circle from light cardboard slightly larger than the cylinder.

2. Cut a strip of fabric 10 mm/½″ wider than the circumference of cylinder and 10 mm/½″ longer than cylinder. Glue it around cylinder so that 10 mm/½″ allowance overlaps neatly around cylinder and 5 mm/¼″ of fabric allowance is folded in at each end of cylinder.

3. Cut a strip of fabric slightly shorter than cylinder length and 10 mm/½″ longer than the circumference of cylinder. Glue strip inside the cylinder.

4. Cut a circle of fabric 5 mm/¼″ larger all around than the base. Glue base onto wrong side of fabric, so that 5 mm/¼″ of fabric hangs free all around. Use scissors to clip V-shapes from fabric allowance. Fold and glue clipped fabric to other side of base.

5. Cut a circle of fabric slightly smaller than the base. Glue fabric in place on uncovered side of base.

6. Run craft glue around the edge of base circle. Fit base into one end of the cylinder and leave to dry.

7. Cut a piece of wadding the same size as lid and glue in place on one side of lid (top side). Cover padded and unpadded side of lid with fabric using the same method as for base.

8. Thread a needle and stitch an invisible starting stitch on lid top. Bring needle up through fabric and through a seed bead. Place needle back down into fabric. Continue to stitch beads at random over the lid top.

9. Stitch an invisible starting stitch in lid rim. Thread bugle bead, a seed bead and another bugle bead. Take a small stitch into the lid rim. Continue stitching beads in this pattern around the lid rim, taking a backstitch between each set of three beads to secure the edging.

DECORATED WOODEN BOXES

FOLK ART DECOUPAGE BOX

YOU WILL NEED:
balsa box
acrylic paint
cut-out pictures from greeting cards
match
pin
clear varnish

1. Thin the paint to a wash consistency with water. Put a coat of paint on the box. A second coat of paint may be applied depending on the depth of colour required. Allow to dry.

2. Glue cut-out pictures of your choice onto the centre of the lid and the box walls.

3. Practise this next step on paper first! Using an unthinned shade of paint darker than the box colour, dip the tail end (not the head) of the match into the paint and make four-dot flowers around the edge of the lid and box.

4. Use a pin head to make the three-dot smaller flower at random over the box. Just dip the pin head in paint and dab on the box three times then re-dip and paint the next flower.

5. Use a pin head and white paint to add another four dots over the centre of each four-dot flower. Also add a white centre to each three-dot flower.

6. Allow paint to dry completely and coat with varnish. Repeat several times on the lid, allowing varnish to dry in between each coat. Varnish can be lightly sanded after each two or three coats. Avoid more than three coats on the box walls underneath the lid rim: too much varnish here will prevent the lid from fitting.

POT POURRI HEART BOX

YOU WILL NEED:
heart-shaped balsa box
acrylic paint
sea sponge
cardboard
organza
ribbon
pot pourri

1. Paint the box inside and out. Allow to dry.

2. Wet the sponge with water and dip it into a contrasting paint colour to the base coat. Dab it onto the box to give a mottled pattern. Apply as much sponged paint as you wish, then allow to dry.

3. Cut a cardboard heart slightly smaller than the box base (use the box to trace around). Check that the heart fits into the box; trim if necessary.

4. Cut a piece of organza about 20 mm/1″ larger all around than the cardboard heart. Place the heart onto the organza and run a line of craft glue around the cardboard, leaving a large gap on one side. Pull the organza onto the cardboard, pressing it into the glue and keeping a gap on one side.

5. Fill the heart with pot pourri through the gap. When filled, glue the gap closed.

6. Fit the pot pourri heart into the box, with cardboard side down.

7. Glue ribbon and bows onto the box using craft glue.

BERIBBONED BOXES

YOU WILL NEED:
set of balsa boxes (various sizes)
tartan, red and green ribbon (different widths)
craft glue

1. Glue lengths of ribbon around the boxes and their lids: wide ribbon on the box and narrow ribbon on the lid.

2. Tie ribbon bows (we used double ribbon) and glue them onto the side or top of each box.

Note: These are wonderful containers for presents of homemade shortbread or chocolates.

RECYCLED BOXES

BOXES COVERED WITH HANDMADE JAPANESE PAPER

YOU WILL NEED:
boxes (soap, chocolate, or any kind of sturdy packaging box)
paper (you can use any other type of paper you desire)
cord or ribbon
spray adhesive or glue stick
brass corners (optional)

1. Cut pieces of paper so that they cover each piece of the box (i.e. lid or base) plus an extra 10 mm/½″ on all sides.

2. Glue appropriate piece of paper to each box piece so that 10 mm/½″ of paper hangs free at each edge. At each corner, use scissors to clip out paper squares from paper allowances. Glue and fold paper to other side of box piece or onto adjoining box piece.

3. Cover each piece in this way, ensuring that any allowances showing on the box are underneath the base or on the inside of the box and lid. If the box has glued tabs, it can be opened, glued flat against the paper then folded and glued together again.

4. Add brass corners, cord and ribbon as desired, using the photograph and instructions for other boxes as a guide.

THREE STORAGE BOXES

You will need:
sturdy shoe boxes
fabric
ribbon
spray adhesive or glue stick
craft glue
acetate or heavy plastic

BOX WITH BOW ON TOP

Note: Use a fold-up type shoe box with tuck-in lid.

1. Unfold the shoe box and unstick any tabs, so the box can lie completely flat.

2. Lie the outside of the box on the wrong side of the fabric. Cut roughly around the box, leaving about 10 mm/½″ all around. Glue the box to fabric and smooth out any wrinkles. Trim neatly around the box edges.

3. Fold the box into the original shape. Glue tabs in place.

4. Glue ribbon around the box, using craft glue. Glue a ribbon bow on top of the box.

BOX WITH WINDOW

Note: Use a standard shoe box.

1. Cut along two corner edges of one end of the shoebox, from the top edge to the base. This forms the end flap.

2. Cut a hole for the window (about 130 mm x 50 mm/5″ x 2″) in the centre of the flap. Cut a piece of fabric 10 mm/½″ larger on all sides than the flap. Glue fabric over outside of flap so that 10 mm/½″ hangs free at each edge of flap. Use scissors to cut out a square of fabric from each corner. Fold and glue allowances to inside of flap. Use scissors to clip the centre of the fabric into the corners of the window hole, then trim so that 10 mm/½″ fabric allowance remains at each edge of the window. Fold the 10 mm/½″ allowance through the window, and glue to inside of flap.

3. Cut a piece of heavy acetate 10 mm/½″ larger on all sides than the window. Glue acetate inside the box to make the window.

4. Take the original shoe box lid and cut the rim off. Place lid on the box and tape it onto the box.

5. Cut a strip of fabric 20 mm/1″ wider and 20 mm/1″ longer than the circumference of the top and bottom of box and the two large sides. Glue it around the box, leaving 10 mm/½″ of fabric free at each end.
Use scissors to clip the allowance at each corner. At the window end, fold and glue the 10 mm/½″ allowance into the box opening. Glue the allowance at the other end onto the box.

6. Cut a piece of fabric slightly smaller than the uncovered end of the box. Glue the piece of fabric in place.

7. Tape one ribbon length to the top edge of the flap and one to the box opening as pictured.

BOX WITH BOW AT SIDE

Note: Use a standard shoe box.

1. Cut a piece of fabric large enough to cover lid top and lid rim plus an extra 10 mm/½″ all around. Glue fabric to lid top. Cut a square of fabric out of each corner. Glue fabric to lid rim and fold and glue allowance inside lid rim.

2. Cut a strip of fabric 20 mm/1″ wider than box walls and 20 mm/1″ longer than the circumference of box walls. Glue the strip around the box so that 10 mm/½″ of fabric hangs free at top and bottom edges and ends overlap neatly. Fold and glue the top fabric allowance to the inside of box. Use scissors to clip the corners of the bottom edge allowance and glue onto the box base.

3. Glue ribbon around the lid and glue a ribbon bow in place.

BUTTON-TOP BOX

YOU WILL NEED:
sturdy box of thin cardboard (e.g. shoe box)
light cardboard
fabric
button with shank
spray adhesive or glue stick
piece of thin cord

1. Trim the box to the size you require, trimming and reconstructing the walls if necessary.

2. Cut a lid piece slightly larger than the top of the box and another cardboard piece slightly smaller than the lid, to line the lid.

3. Cut cardboard liner pieces for the box slightly smaller than the walls and the base.

4. Cut a strip of fabric 20 mm/1″ wider and 10 mm/½″ longer than the walls. Glue around the box walls so that 10 mm/½″ of fabric hangs free at top and bottom edges, and ends overlap neatly. At each corner of bottom allowance, use scissors to clip fabric in to the edge of the cardboard. Fold and glue allowances to inside of box and onto base.

5. Cut a piece of fabric 10 mm/½″ larger on all sides than lid. Glue onto lid so that 10 mm/½″ of fabric hangs free at each edge of lid. Use scissors to clip out a small square of fabric at each corner. Fold and glue the fabric allowance to other side of lid. Pierce a hole through the centre of the covered side of lid and insert the shank of the button. Thread a thin cord piece through the button shank and tape it under the lid.

6. Use the same method as described above to cover lid liner and glue in place on the underside of the lid.

7. Use the same method to cover the wall and base liners and glue liners into the box.

TWO-DRAWER BOX

YOU WILL NEED:
four same-size boxes such as cereal boxes, two with
top flap attached to form drawers
light cardboard
fabric
spray adhesive or glue stick

1. Cut one narrow end, e.g. top flap of cereal box, from two boxes. Glue one box on top of the other, so that open ends are at the same end. (This section will hold the two drawers.)

2. Cut a strip of fabric as long as the length of the narrow end of the box and 20 mm/1″ wide. Glue this fabric strip across the edge where the open ends of boxes meet; between the drawers.

3. To cover the top and bottom and two large sides, cut a strip of fabric 20 mm/ 1″ wider than box and 20 mm/1″ longer than the circumference of the top and bottom and two large sides. Glue it around the box so that 10 mm/½″ of fabric hangs free at the edges of the opening at front and at the back edges (opposite end to opening). Use scissors to clip the 10 mm/½″ allowance at front opening edges where the boxes meet and at the corners of front opening and the back. Fold and glue allowance inside the box at the front opening and onto the back. Cut a rectangle of fabric the same size as the back of the box. Glue in place.

4. Cut one large side, e.g. the front of a cereal box, from one of the remaining boxes to form a drawer. (This box should still have its top flap attached. Trim it so that it fits inside one of the openings in the main box (one side may need to be cut off, trimmed, then re-attached with tape to make the drawer fit). Tape top flap of box closed to form a drawer. Tape all corners to reinforce the drawer.

5. Cut a strip of fabric the same width as the drawer walls and the same length as circumference of drawer walls. Cut a piece of fabric the same size as the base of drawer. Glue wall piece to the inside of box walls, then glue in base cover.

6. Cut a piece of fabric 20 mm/1″ wider than the walls and 10 mm/½″ longer than the circumference of the walls. Glue around walls so that 10 mm/½″ of fabric hangs free at top and bottom edges and ends overlap neatly. At each corner of bottom fabric allowance use scissors to clip fabric in to cardboard. Fold and glue the fabric allowance inside drawer walls and onto base of drawer.

7. Make the second drawer in the same way.

8. Cut two strips of fabric for drawer tabs 30 mm/1½″ wide and the length you desire. Fold each strip in half, right-side out, to form tab, tucking edges inside and gluing in place. Centre each tab at the top edge of front of drawer and glue in place. Glue a piece of fabric over tape to conceal it.

LIST OF BOXES

FABRIC BOXES

The most impressive decorative boxes
are those covered with beautiful fabrics.
Match fabrics with decor, add
embroidery, patchwork or even quilting
– here's your chance to be really creative.
(See instructions starting on page 31.)

EASY HAT BOX

SET OF TRIANGULAR BOXES

PADDED HAT BOXES

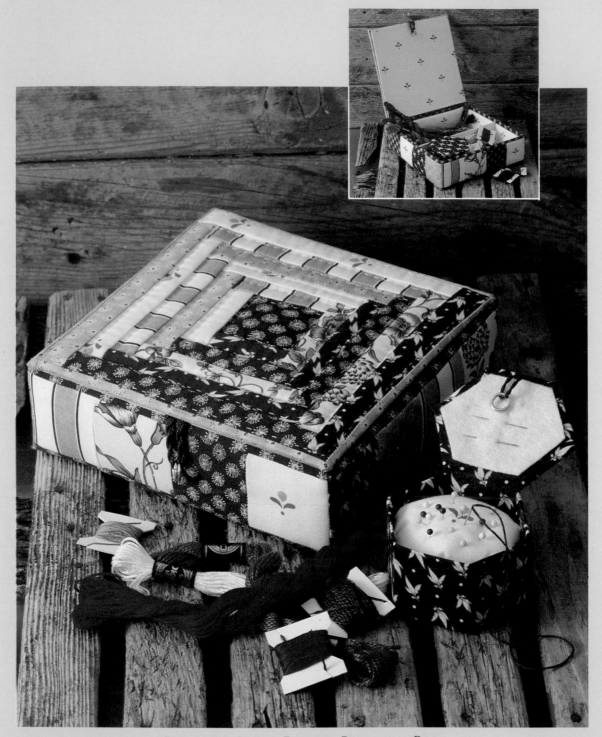

PATCHWORK SEWING BOX WITH PINCUSHION BOX

CUTWORK BOX

LOVELY LACQUERED BOXES – ROUND AND SQUARE

BEADED RING BOX

GATHERED AND PADDED JEWELLERY BOX AND BOX WITH PLEATED LID

Decorated Wooden Boxes

Take simple balsa boxes and add paint,
paper, ribbons and trims. In no time
you'll have a charming set of boxes; the
scented heart in this chapter is
everyone's favourite.
(See instructions starting on page 53.)

Folk Art Decoupage Box

POT POURRI HEART BOX

BERIBBONED BOXES

RECYCLED BOXES

Make something from nothing! Save
shoe boxes and chocolate boxes and
convert them into beautiful gift and
storage boxes.
(See instructions starting on page 57.)

BOXES COVERED WITH HANDMADE JAPANESE PAPER

THREE STORAGE BOXES

TWO-DRAWER BOX AND BUTTON-TOP BOX

ACKNOWLEDGEMENTS

Writing a craft book is a time-consuming exercise but made easier with help from family and friends, whether it be physical assistance or, more importantly, positive encouragement.

I'd like to thank the people who have helped with this book. Especially Rodney, who took the photographs, and Sharne, who was so enthusiastic about the project. Maria and Joy have given positive encouragement from the very beginning and Maryanne and Robbylee have offered valuable advice.

A big thank you to Lisa for her enthusiasm and to the other 'craft girls' – Claire, Lesley, Kestie, Lesley, Sharon and Isobel – who spur me on.

And special thanks to my publishers, Sally and Marg, and to Metta, who took over the housework and cooking while I made boxes.

CREDITS

Linen and Lace of Balmain and Cottage and Lace of Bondi Junction provided many of the props in this book. I am grateful for their cooperation.